Dr. Debi Toporoff

Debi is one of the most amazing examples of God's redemptive power I have ever met. When all circumstances demanded defeat, she came out victorious. Not only did she escape the hopelessness of the life she once knew, but also she is truly enjoying herself each and every day! Only God could make such a transformation.

—JONNA LEDYAEV
MISSIONARY TO RUSSIA

A compelling and riveting true story of overcoming child abuse, both mental and physical, and the long road to recovery and success. This book will be required reading for any professional who deals with children.

—SHARON SIGURDSON
RETIRED SCHOOLTEACHER

It is with great joy that I give my support to Dr. Debi Toporoff's new book *Oops! Wrong Family*. It has moved my heart and challenged my emotions. I believe anyone who reads this book will be touched with compassion for others and motivated within to make it in spite of the stormy circumstances of life

—REVEREND DR. DONALD R. JORDAN
TRINITY CHRISTIAN METHODIST EPISCOPAL CHURCH
AUGUSTA, GEORGIA

OOPS!

Wrong Family

Debi Toporoff

CREATION
HOUSE
A STRANG COMPANY

OOPS! WRONG FAMILY by Debi Toporoff
Published by Creation House
A Strang Company
600 Rinehart Road
Lake Mary, Florida 32746
www.creationhouse.com

Unless otherwise marked, all Scripture quotations are from the Holy Bible, New International Version. Copyright © 1973, 1978, 1984, International Bible Society. Used by permission.

Scripture quotations marked KJV are from the King James Version of the Bible.

This book is a work of non-fiction. Names and places have been changed to protect the privacy of individuals. The events and situations are all true.

Cover design by Terry Clifton

Library of Congress Control Number: 2005932816
International Standard Book Number: 1-59185-916-6

First Edition

06 07 08 09 — 987654321
Printed in the United States of America

To Paul Mispel Sr., who rescued me every time he could and loved me enough to know there was something more for my life than hurt, heartache, and abandonment. Thank you, Grandpa, for being yourself.

Also to my Uncle Glen and Aunt Mary Frank Carr who were, and still are, my heroes. I love you all very much.

Acknowledgments

MY HEARTFELT THANKS to Roger and Tobie Stitt for their patience, and for seeing in me a person when I did not even know what a person was.

Uncle Glenn and Aunt Mary Frank Carr, for being my heroes, for their prayers, and the example of their Christian walk before our family. Thank you both for being there and loving me through the good times and the bad.

Pat Simmons for taking up for me when others thought I was a misfit. You showed unconditional love when I was not lovable.

Bill and Sharon Sigurdson, for going against the grain and believing in me through the years. I love you—and yes I know, ditto!

Phil and Betty Newton, for their great sense of humor

and knowing how to love people back to life when their heart is dead.

Nita Canoy, for your spunk, advice, and willingness to speak the truth regardless of the consequences.

Paul and Glyndal Mispel—my father and stepmother—who did the best they knew how to raise an already dysfunctional family. Thank you for the privilege of allowing me a small part in your lives.

May the Lord add great blessings to your lives and families. I can never repay any of you for what you gave me. But, I will pass it on.

Contents

Introduction

IF IT WAS possible to inspect your new family before birth, some of us might choose a different family. Everyone has memories from childhood and we often try to guard those memories, both good and bad, in our hearts. Over time, the memories shape our character and even our destiny in life.

The incidents in this book are true. The first few chapters specifically have been written from a child's point of view to describe what a child might have thought up to the age of three. This book was not written to entertain. Its purpose is to let other survivors know there is life after abuse. We cannot change the past, but we can change the memories in our hearts so that we can become whole in God's sight and in our own right. I hope this book encourages you.

This is the story of the abuse in my childhood. It is also the story of recovery—a life that went from hurt, to hope, to healing. I found that Jesus is the answer to my problems, and that in forgiveness there is freedom.

To God be the glory—for His mercy, grace, and abundant patience in my life.

Chapter 1

THE SMELL OF fish was stinking up the fish house as the sun rose and the fishermen were in their boats. They were picking mullet, shiners, pompano, and various other fish out of their nets. One day, my daddy got stuck by a stingray and the poison made a hole in his ankle. The poison traveled up his leg and came out his knee. He could not go fishing for a long time.

Each fisherman had a tale to tell of their day on the river or the ocean. Some of the womenfolk brought food and drink to the men, but it seemed that my mama never had time to bring Daddy something to eat. She was too busy with other things, but I never knew what. The other fishermen always shared their food with Daddy as if they understood his situation.

Very few folks in town had much money to speak of and

everybody knew everyone else. Gossip seemed to sweep the town quicker than a snake striking at a rabbit. If someone was hungry, Daddy gave their family some fish, as did the other fishermen. My dad even paid the doctor's bill in fish because real money was scarce. Everyone in the town liked to barter for what they needed because hardly anyone had any money.

My daddy had big dreams of playing quarterback for some professional football team one day, but his dreams were shattered when the girl he was dating became pregnant. He figured the honorable thing to do was to get married. Why not? She was the prettiest girl in school, and she was a majorette. Daddy was the captain of his high school football team. He could run like the wind and throw a football farther than anyone else. Little did he know that he should have run from his soon-to-be bride. He was voted Best All-Around in his yearbook each year.

Daddy had light brown hair and blue eyes that twinkled when he laughed, like he didn't have a care in the world. Anyone who knew him had only good things to say about him. If there were fish to be found in the ocean, he found them and hauled 'em on in. He never went out in his boat without coming home with some kind of fish. And yet, no one would have guessed the hidden secrets that were in his home.

Jenny, later to be known as my mother, was another story. With blonde hair, blue eyes, and a slender build, she was the type most men gawked at. But she had her eye on Daddy, and whatever Jenny set her sights on she usually got.

Her character was very different from Daddy's, maybe even a little strange. In public she was the life of the party, but behind closed doors there raged a heart of hurt, bitterness, and abandonment. No matter how much my dad tried to love or provide for her, it never seemed to be enough. The neighbors heard them arguing for days at a time. Daddy was often seen walking barefoot down the dirt road toward the fish house to find a little peace and solitude.

Not long after their marriage came Marie, their first in a long line of children. Marie was a small baby with a few strands of hair. Ten fingers and ten toes, all body parts were present and accounted for. Jenny now had someone she possibly could love who might love her back. There was only one problem—babies have to be taught love before they can give it. You cannot give away what you don't have or haven't learned.

It was not long afterward that Jenny found herself pregnant with a second child, but this child was not wanted. It wasn't because of the timing, but because the identity of the father was not known. From what could be gathered, this child was from one of seven fathers. Only God knew who the real father was at that time.

Jenny's lifestyle had become one of secrecy. When my dad went fishing, men came to her door like a bunch of vultures. They sure weren't selling pots and pans, according to the information I later received. The funny thing about these men was that they had one thing in common with my father: they were fishermen. It seemed that everyone but my dad knew about these flings. But aren't those in the family always the last to know, or was Daddy just overlooking her behavior? Even Grandpa knew of her promiscuous behavior and for this my mother hated him.

Jenny also hated Grandpa because he didn't mince his words when he had something to say. Grandpa had that tough, German heritage in which he not only worked hard, but was also hardheaded.

Oops! Wrong Family

Grandpa was only five-feet-eight inches tall, but when he spoke he sometimes sounded like thunder. His hard exterior only gave way to his marshmallow heart when he came to my rescue many times in the following years. He made the best homemade root beer in the world. It had a lot of bubbles in it and it made my face all tingly. He could even write the Lord's Prayer on half of a postage stamp. He made lamps and jewelry and potholders out of shells he found on the beach to support himself. The stories he told kept me coming back for more.

Meanwhile, in the womb a baby struggled to get comfortable.

> *What's this? I can't stretch out in this bubble machine. What's that sound? Who's there? The voice is saying that I am fearfully and wonderfully made (Ps. 139:14), and that He knew me in my mother's womb (Jer. 1:5). That's silly, how can anyone know me? I haven't been born yet. Where did that voice come from? Maybe it was some water monster trying to be funny. Guess I'll just swish around in this swimming pool and suck my thumb. Nothing else to do in here...*

"Paul, the baby is moving," Jenny said excitedly. "Put your hand right here."

Daddy knew in his heart that the kick he felt was his child. I could hear his soothing from within the warm swimming pool that was my home for a while. He talked to me for a long time and moved his hand all over her belly just to get another kick from me, but I got tired and drifted off to sleep. A sudden jolt woke me up to strange noises, which I later came to know as yelling.

This person carrying me could be heard sobbing and then cursing for being pregnant. I heard harsh sounds in my protected environment and then a swat on top of her belly could be felt. I thought it was strange that I was hurt when she swatted her belly and then cursed. *Must be some sort of game*, I thought. Whoever said an unborn child couldn't feel or hear things outside was wrong. I could tell that this person carrying me didn't want me. I sure didn't want to meet this person, but we were destined to anyway.

Wow! Who caused a leak in my swimming pool? I'm sliding, but I don't want to get out yet. It's bad out there. Hey, Voice in here who said I'm wonderfully made—don't make me go out there. Ooooh! That thing is cold on my head. I'm freezing. Put me back where it's warm and safe. Put me back. Somebody's got me, but they look like an alien. Another alien in white just slapped my little butt, put me in this soft fuzzy thing, and handed me to this other alien in white. Hey, this feels nice and warm. I wonder if I can snuggle to the bottom of this fuzzy thing.

Laying in that bucket thing, or *crib* as the hospital called it, I had a few minutes to think. How was a girl to get out of this mess? The lady in white wiped all that sticky stuff off of me, and that man in the mask over there started poking me. I guess he wanted to see if I was alive, so I hollered in his ear when he put me over his shoulder. I guess he knows who's boss now!

There is a lady in white that people here call *nurse*, but her real name is Mary. She picked me up in her arms and took me to see the lady who housed me in that warm swimming pool for a long time. I thought she would be glad to see me, but when Mary tried to lay me down beside her, Jenny started screaming, "Get her out of here! She looks like her grandfather! I don't want her—get her out of here right now!"

What did I do?

The nurse held me close and said, "I don't know why she doesn't want you. You're a beautiful child." Yeah, I was kinda cute with my bald head and baby blues looking up at this kind nurse holding me. I had ten fingers and ten toes, and it looked like everything else worked, too. I was given the name Debi and became the favorite baby in the nursery, but I really didn't know why.

All the other babies had people oohing and aahing over them, but I only had the nurses and doctors. Where were the folks that were supposed to make a fuss over me? Where's Daddy Paul? (That's what the nurses called those funny, awkward men trying to hold their newborn babies in their arms—*daddy*). Daddy never came, and the lady that housed me never came either. She just left the hospital and didn't even come see me.

A couple of days went by and I watched the other babies leave the nursery in peoples' arms. The grown-ups were laughing and kissing each other as they left with their little bundles of joy. It seemed that as my playmates left, others came in to take their place.

The nursery was noisy with all of us making a racket at the same time. Those were the good old days, laying around, eating and sleeping, then getting rewarded by the nurse sticking something to eat in our mouths from time to time. That goo didn't taste too bad, either. All I had to do was make a loud noise and the nurse would come over and talk to me and take care of me. She sometimes sang a song that went like this:

Jesus loves me, this I know.
For the Bible tells me so.
Little ones to Him belong,
They are weak, but He is strong.
Yes, Jesus loves me.
Yes, Jesus loves me.
Yes, Jesus loves me,
The Bible tells me so.

When she sang that song to me I felt safe in her arms and easily fell asleep. But who was Jesus, I wanted to know? Daddy Paul and Jenny didn't come back for me, and I began to wonder if something was wrong with me.

Why didn't they want me?

Chapter 2

Who's that new lady? She's not a nurse because she doesn't have white on like Mary. They said she is a social worker, but I don't know what a social worker is. What's she saying to that doctor over there? She keeps pointing at me and then she says something about a foster home. Maybe that is my family's name, because I heard other babies being called a name. I can be a "foster," but I don't know about that "home" part. That sounds funny.

Before long, that lady came into the nursery and walked over to my bucket with Mary. The sides of her mouth went up to the sky as she bent over me. *What are you looking at me for?* I wondered. Her name was Miss Golda. She looked old because she had baggy skin on her face and her cheeks were red. Her hair was tied up in a big ball on the back of her head. When she picked me up, her hands were warm and the sides of her mouth went up when she talked to me. I thought I even saw a twinkling star in her eyes. So, Miss Golda is what they call a social worker.

Miss Golda said, "I don't know why they didn't want you, but I have a family that wants a baby very badly. They are good people, and they will love you and take care of you," she said as she placed me back in my bucket and kissed my forehead.

That felt yucky but good at the same time. *Come back and kiss me on the forehead again, right here,* I cried, but they just said, "Listen to that child scream. She sure does have a set of lungs on her." Then they laughed as they left the nursery. I thought I saw Miss Golda turn around and smile at me. Maybe there's nothing wrong with me after all. Somebody actually wants me!

Miss Golda picked me up from the hospital nursery one day to take me to the foster family, but I later found out that a foster home was not a family's name but a place where kids are put when their family doesn't want them. This family's name was Burger. They had a farm in Indiantown, Florida. They were a kindly family, I was told later, and I got lots of hugs and kisses there. They also had this gray pony, and they let me ride on it with Papa Burger. I was what they called a toddler when they let me on the pony. At night, Mama Burger sang to me. Papa Burger gave me a big hug before putting me in the crib. It felt so good when he held me in those big arms. I never got tired of being safe in Papa Burger's lap.

As a toddler, I had fun getting into all sorts of things like pots and pans, Mama Burger's shoes, dirt piles, and mud puddles. I liked the mud puddles the best because they felt squishy on my feet and tasted good, too. I also liked to bang on the pots and pans. It drove the big people bonkers. Mama Burger would say, "Debi, you are going to be the death of me yet," then tickle me a whole lot and laugh. I tried to get in her way when she was washing dishes to play in the soapsuds. I liked Papa Burger the best because I got to ride on the tractor with him and play with the horses.

By then I was a big kid, all twenty-seven pounds of me at almost two years old. Potty training was a trip until I got some big people underwear. For some reason, every time I went potty they gave me a big cookie. Potty, then cookie—it didn't sound bad to me. Besides, I now had *them* trained. Making crumbs was the most fun, but I had to eat the cookie outside so Mama Burger wouldn't have to sweep the floor again.

Mama and Papa Burger talked to Miss Golda to see if they could adopt me. Miss Golda told them the chances were pretty slim because the mother (my mother) was going back to court to try to get me back. Miss Golda told them that Debi's father said that he and his wife had decided they wanted their baby to live with them. I really didn't understand what that meant, but from the look on Papa and Mama Burgers' faces I knew something was not right. The social workers back then believed that a child should be with their natural family at any cost—even to the detriment of the child.

I didn't want to go with them. I had it good here. Why couldn't I just stay with Mama and Papa Burger? I didn't know those strange people, and don't little kids have a choice, anyway? Who is that blonde-haired lady and the man in the yard with Miss Golda? They just kept walking closer and closer to the house. Then I recognized them as the people who left me at the hospital and didn't even come see me. Why did they want to see me now?

Oops! Wrong Family

They acted as if they knew me, but I sure didn't want to know them. They told Mama and Papa Burger that they would pick me up on the weekend to go and live with them...but I already had a mama and papa. I didn't want anyone else. They bent down to pick me up, but I'm sure I ran away in my hot-shot diaper.

The rest of the week was very sad for Mama and Papa Burger. They cried every time they looked at me or held me in their arms. I started to think I had done something wrong. It was very hard for them the day I had to go. I went kicking and screaming with my teddy bear tucked under one arm and a soggy cookie in my other hand. Who would have thought that I would never see them again? I suppose I was the death of them after all.

I screamed and hollered all the way home. They kept telling me it was going to be okay and that there were lots of toys at home to play with. There were dolls and balls and lots of things, but there wasn't a big tractor or horses to play with. There wasn't even Mama or Papa Burger to get hugs and kisses from in the new house. They also told me I had a big sister and a little brother, whoever they were.

Sure enough I found out what a big sister was. She was the one who pulled my hair and took my toys. Sometimes she was nice to me. She was three years old at the time. My little brother just crawled around and cried a lot. He was 364 days younger than me.

I still missed Mama and Papa Burger. I cried a lot because I missed them, but after a while the memory of them began to fade. I just felt a hurt in my heart but didn't know why.

This family was named Mispel and that was the name I was born with. Mama Mispel never gave me hugs or kisses and she never sang to me at night. When I cried she just hit me and yelled at me to shut up. When she yelled, she said she would see to it that I would never have a home and then she called me a nobody.

I learned how to roll up in a ball whenever Mama Mispel came near me so it wouldn't hurt so much if she hit me or kicked me. I stopped playing with the toys and laughing or even playing with Sissy or my little brother. A short time later, Mama Mispel tied me in a swing all day because I wasn't good enough to play. I messed my pants, but it just stayed there until dark when I was brought inside, bathed, fed, and put to bed. Sometimes she held my head underwater and laughed. Grandpa caught her doing that one day and grabbed her by the hair and screamed at her. He sure was mad that day. Grandpa even changed my dirty diapers when he came to the house. He scrubbed me so good that I thought my butt was going to never-never land.

Daddy Paul came home from fishing and gave me a big hug and told me he loved me. Daddy sure was stinky after fishing all day. Was that what fishing smelled like? I wondered if he knew what Mama was really like. I wished she could be more like him.

Sometimes I heard Grandpa and Mama yelling at each other, and most of the time the arguments were over me and how to take care of me. Grandpa got mad at her and then he untied me from the swing and let me sit in his lap. He didn't even mind cleaning me up when I was dirty. Grandpa never yelled at me when I messed my britches or cried too hard. Between the dirt and tears it was a wonder Grandpa even knew who I was. It didn't matter to Grandpa because he loved me and protected me. He was my hero and I looked forward to his visits.

Oops! Wrong Family

One day, I must have made Mama mad because she hit me with her hand and then threw me across the room. I landed on the cement, but I couldn't get up and I began screaming and screaming. It really hurt a lot. I must have done something wrong to make her that mad. She got mad a whole lot, but she never got mad at Sissy or my little brother. They ran into another room and peeked around the corner in order to see what was going to happen to their sister. Mama started yelling for me to get up, but the harder I tried the more it hurt. At two years old, I didn't understand what was happening and wished Daddy or Grandpa was there.

Mama had to take me to the hospital and told the nurses that I fell in a hole and wasn't watching where I was going. I heard the nurses talking about Mama. They said this was the third time since I went to live with them that I had come in with bruises, and this time my leg was broken and I had a goose egg on the back of my head. I was afraid of the nurses because they poked something in my little behind to take my temperature. It sure hurt and I pitched a royal fit, but it didn't hurt me as much as Mama had. My squirming probably didn't help much, either. They also had this needle way up to the sky, and the lady in white held me down when that man jabbed me with it. She kept telling me it would be all right, but I just kept screaming.

The doctor put a big, heavy sheet around my leg, and then put white mud all over it. Later I learned that the big white sheet and white mud were a cast they used to keep the broken portion of my leg in place. The nurse held me real close while the doctor fixed my leg. I had to stay at the hospital a couple of days. Funny thing was, even though I was afraid of Mama, I still screamed a long time for her after she left. *How come she left me?* I wondered.

The other moms stayed with their kids, and one of the kids had his daddy there, too. Speaking of Daddy, where was he? Oh, I forgot, he had to go fishing and bring home some more money for Mama. Everyone called her a roadrunner…at least, that's what Daddy said.

The nurses had a hard time calming me down so this one nurse, Jennifer, took me in her arms in the rocking chair and started singing:

> Jesus loves the little children,
> All the little children of the world.
> Red and yellow, black and white,
> They are precious in His sight.
> Jesus loves the little children of the world.

She kept singing it over and over, and before long I just laid in her lap and listened to her sing. Who was this Jesus she sang about? This lady must have read my mind when she said, "Jesus loves you very much and He will take care of you." If He was taking care of me, how come I was all broken up and I'm just a little kid with ten fingers and ten toes?

Over the next couple of days I became the nurses' favorite. I heard them talking about Mama, but neither she nor Daddy came to see me. Jennifer kept singing that Jesus song each time she took care of me, but I sure couldn't figure out who the "yellow children" were. Where does the yellow kid live? And how did he get yellow? That yellow kid wasn't in my bed or anywhere around the room. If I just knew grown-up talk I would have asked her. Maybe she could learn toddler talk? Then we could tell each other stories. That would be fun.

Mama finally came to the hospital to get me after the nurse called her and told her to. My sister Marie came with her and had a big teddy bear. She was three-and-a-half-years-old and could talk grown-up talk. I wondered if she could ask Mama what yellow children were. Mama had a big smile on her face, but it only lasted in the hospital. She didn't seem too happy—sad face–glad face, glad face–sad face, *that* was Mama.

Everybody seemed nice to me for the next couple of weeks. Miss Golda popped in to check on the family at least twice a week and Mama was always so very nice. Marie and Mike (that's my little brother) were allowed to play with me when Miss Golda came by. Marie even shared her dolls with me. I really liked the rag doll called Annie because I could hold her close and feel the softness of her hair. *Maybe I'm not so bad after all,* I thought. Marie, Mike, and I watched *Roadrunner* cartoons on the black-and-white television. I wanted to be like the Roadrunner and run as fast as my little legs would carry me…all the way to Daddy's boat.

I missed him.

Chapter 3

Mama's being nice didn't last very long. One day, Grandpa was at our house watching us so Mama could go out again. She was dressed all pretty in her dress and smelled kinda yucky. I began crying real loud in my high chair, I don't remember why, but the louder I cried the madder Mama got. I must have been a real crybaby that day. Mama kept yelling for me to shut up, but I couldn't. The more she yelled the louder I squalled. Mama became a wild animal and began hitting me again and again until her wedding ring missed my head and went into my left eye. She swung at me again, but there was now blood coming from my eye and my forehead. I was about two-and-a-half years old when that happened.

Grandpa went into a rage. Mama ran out to the car and locked herself in. Grandpa tried to grab her out of the car, but she just sped off with the tires squealing. Grandpa came in and cleaned the blood off my face and held me real close because I couldn't quit crying, and didn't understand what happened. My eye and head hurt and I couldn't do anything about it. Grandpa didn't have a way to get me to the hospital and there wasn't a phone at our house. Mama didn't take me to the hospital until the next day.

At the hospital, they gave me a teddy bear that I could cuddle up to. I heard Mama say she would not sign for my eye to be fixed. Didn't Daddy care? Where was he? I found out later that I would have been able to see with two eyes if Mama would have signed to let the eye doctor fix it. The doctor said he would have to call the social worker and have me taken out of the home. When he said that, Mama just spun around on her heels and left without saying good-bye. I started screaming—*Come back Mama! Don't go! I'll be good!* But she didn't even look back.

When Jennifer came on, I was still crying. She picked me up and held me close, and began singing and rocking me to sleep. She sang a lot of songs, but I liked that one about Jesus and the yellow children the best. She told me stories about little lambs and sheep. Jennifer spent a lot of time with me over the next month or so. She even came in sometimes when she wasn't scheduled. Jennifer became my "bestest" friend in the whole world.

A funny cup was placed over my left eye and a string was placed over my right eye. The nurses kept putting socks on my hands so I wouldn't pull things apart. Sometimes the nurses made a smiley face on my sock and pretended the sock was talking like some sort of monkey or puppy. I thought the hospital was going to be my new home because I had been there forever.

Then one day, I looked up to see Miss Golda standing there. She always showed up when I least expected it. Today she had on a red and white dress with some glittery stuff on it. She came over to my crib and began to talk and tickled me. It made me laugh and she still had that twinkle in her eye like Santa Claus. She told me about this teacher, Mrs. Fink, who wanted to take me home. She didn't have any children of her own and her husband liked kids. They also visited me every day. One day, they brought me ice cream and I made a mess eating it. They just laughed and didn't even get mad.

Mrs. Fink wore funny hats when she went to the store or work, or just to a friend's house. She was about five-foot-two, but to me she looked like a giant. When she held me, she felt squishy and I just snuggled into her.

That's the way little kids should feel—safe from everything.

She had red hair and hazel eyes that danced when she smiled or laughed. When she walked she bounced like a ball tumbling down the road. Mr. Fink was taller than the tallest tree and was real skinny. When the wind blew, it messed up his brown hair or made his hat fly off his head. That always made me laugh, but I think he made his hat fall off on purpose just to hear me giggle. He gave me piggyback rides on his shoulders and I wrapped my little arms real tight around his neck so I wouldn't fall off. *That* was fun.

Mr. and Mrs. Fink lived on a dirt road behind the fish house. They took me to Mr. Po's soda shop and bought me ice cream on Sunday after church. You know, I heard that song about Jesus and the yellow children there, too. The preacher talked about Jesus loving little children and how they came up to

Him in the Bible. I just wished He could talk to me like that. He's not like Papa or Mama Fink. Mama Fink says He's real.

Living with them was good. My nightmares seemed to lessen over time, but I was still known for the best temper tantrums the world had ever seen. I stayed at Mama and Papa Fink's for the next two years. Like any little girl, I had Papa Fink wrapped around my little finger.

Every once in a while I saw my Daddy on his boat, laughing with the other fishermen. I was sure if he saw me he would pick me up in his arms and give me a big huggy-bear hug.

Daddy, why can't you see me? Don't you know who I am anymore? Do you ever think about me and wonder if I'm okay? You catch more fish than anyone, but you can't seem to hold on to me. I saw you out there fixing your net after a shark bit a big old hole in it…or were you out there to stay away from Mama? Daddy, please come over and fix this hole right here in my heart…

…then I cried but didn't really know why, and my little heart felt like it was going to break. I felt the Wind, and sometimes it talked to me. The Wind said, "I still have My hand on you, My child." Then I got this warm feeling inside my heart just for a moment.

At the end of the two years with Mama and Papa Fink, they went to court to adopt me. My daddy said Mama had changed when she found out the Fink family wanted to adopt me. She didn't want me, but she didn't want anybody else to have me, either. At least she was true to her word about making sure I never had a home.

When the social worker said, "Pack your bags, you're going

to another place," it really meant your opinion did not count. You had to be twelve-years-old for the judge to ask you where you wanted to live. Little kids like me had opinions too, didn't we? If there was ever anything called toddler depression, I'm sure I had it.

For some reason the judge believed Daddy and Mama, and a piece of my heart became like stone when Miss Golda came and got me. But this time I left Mama and Papa Fink's house kicking and screaming. It was as if someone was trying to kill me—and emotionally they did. Mama and Papa Fink also cried when they watched me being put in the car. That must have really been hard for them. How was I to know that four years later she would be my third-grade teacher?

By now there was another kid in the family, but I was still the outcast. When chores were to be done, I had to do them. I was only four years old, but someone had to wash the dirty diapers in the commode or mop the house or even wash the window screens outside in the dark. When it rained, Mama put me out of the house and locked the door so I couldn't get back in, especially when it was thundering and lightning. She stood at the door and laughed at me crying and begging her to let me in. When she let me in, she hit me for getting my clothes wet. The next time she threw me out in the rain, I hid in the doghouse to try not to get my clothes wet. That made Mama angry and you sure didn't want to make Mama angry no matter what. Later, the rain and lightning became my friends because I was no longer afraid of them, but I still didn't like the thunder. Daddy always said thunder was from giants playing marbles in heaven. Those must have been some pretty big marbles.

Oops! Wrong Family

For the next two or three years the abuse continued and the number of kids in the family continued to grow. Whose kids they actually were we will never know because of all the men Mama dated while Daddy was out fishing. By now, Mama and Daddy slept in different bedrooms, but if she thought she was pregnant she went in and stayed the night with Daddy. Did he know he was being used? Probably, but it didn't matter.

The day came when Mama's games of hit the nobody, scream at the nobody, and kick the nobody came to an end for a short while. She hit me so hard that my skull split in two places. She told the hospital staff that I fell off my bike trying to do those tricks kids do. She seemed to fidget as the questions were asked about how the accident happened.

The same doctor and nurses were at the hospital when I came in with the hurt eye. The doctor reported the abuse again, and I saw Miss Golda. The only difference this time was that I didn't cry or speak to anyone. They couldn't even make me laugh at things normal kids thought were funny. I somehow had created my own safe place away from the world of hurt, broken promises, and lies. I had no laughter in my heart anymore…just rocks, because rocks don't get hurt. My heart was now as hard as a rock, so I thought no one would ever be able to get to me now. The doctor sewed up my head and I didn't even cry.

"Did any of my brains come out?" I asked. The doctor just laughed and let me know that I still had all my brains.

I had to stay in the hospital for a while, but I had a big people's bed to sleep in. Nurse Mary no longer worked at the hospital because she got hitched to this lawyer and moved away, but I didn't know where. By now, the Jesus loves the little children song was embedded deep in my brain, but my heart could not believe anybody could love me—not even Jesus.

Miss Golda showed up before the doctor finished sewing up my head. I sure knew what that meant; I had been down that road before. She visited me every day while looking for a home for me to go to. The next set of foster parents couldn't even get through to me. At night, I cried when no one was looking—if someone saw you crying you got hit and then you would get laughed at for being a crybaby. My heart and skin were becoming like shark's skin: rough, hard, impossible for others to get through. I was known as a tough kid by the age of six.

I was at those foster parents' home for a couple of weeks before being sent back into my parent's home. I couldn't even remember the foster parents' names, but I'm sure they tried to get through to me. Funny, I didn't even cry this time when I left that foster home. By now I had learned what to expect at Mama's which was nothing but hurt, abandonment, and rejection.

So began the saga of foster home-to-foster home. If the kids at school found out you were a foster kid you became an outcast. The other kids made fun of you for not having a mother or father. They could be so cruel at times, but they just didn't understand…

> …all a foster kid wanted was just to be accepted for who she was…to have somebody to play with.

After two more years and several more foster homes, my real parents again went to the judge and told him that Mama had changed. It took a little more convincing this time because the judge had heard that same story several times before. Mama had learned the art of conning men and she was a master of storytelling. Whatever she told the judge worked. My bags were put in the back of their car.

It was not long after being back there that Mama began her games again. When she came home after being out wherever it was she had been, she woke me up and made me sit outside by the woods all night. I imagined all sorts of things in the woods that could get me, and sometimes I wished the things in the woods would come get me because I would be away from Mama and her wicked games.

I was told that the *gooptagallopers* and the *wampas bats* would get me if I moved from where she made me sit. What those were I didn't know, but I kept my eyes out for them all night. I cried until I fell asleep in that spot, wishing for day-light to come soon.

Daylight couldn't come soon enough, with all the sounds in the night air. Mama must have really hated me because, no matter the weather, I spent many nights in the edge of the woods. When she was in a good mood, I got a blanket in the wintertime; if not, I didn't get anything but the clothes I had on. I welcomed the winter, though. The snakes were gone and I didn't have to be so afraid. Funny how Mama let me sleep in the house if Daddy was home. I wished he had been home more often.

Come morning, she made me do the chores before school, like ironing the clothes, washing the dirty diapers in the com-mode, washing the dishes, and mopping the floor. If they weren't done to her satisfaction she hit me in the head or my back while yelling how stupid I was and how she wished I was dead. She must have really hated me for reminding her every day of the fling she had that brought about my existence. She must have hated that man, too. I wondered who that person was, but I still looked like my grandpa. That was okay by me because that meant I looked like somebody, even though I felt like a nobody.

Nobodies have feelings too, don't they? So why do I feel so numb?

If I didn't finish my chores before the school bus came I wasn't allowed to go to school. Sometimes I ran through the woods when I missed the school bus just to be safe at school for a few hours. I didn't even stop to put on my shoes, knowing that if I got caught there would be big trouble. This enraged Mama because it gave me the upper hand—at least for a few hours. That sure was short lived. She often came to the school and got me out of class saying I had a doctor's appointment or some other lame excuse, knowing it was a lie. Did the school officials know her games or did they truly believe her? On the way home she made me sit in the front seat so she could curse at me and hit me at the same time for trying to go to school against her wishes. What she didn't know was that I did this again and again just for a few hours of safety.

After living in such awful conditions for any length of time you begin to believe it is normal and that every family had one kid that was the scapegoat or black sheep of the family. I was the nobody that nobody wanted and I thought nobody would ever love. It was amazing how many people knew what was happening in that house, but never said a word or lifted a finger to change the situation.

Elementary school became my haven because of the safety

there, but there were also problems at school. I was called "Old One Eye" and all sorts of other names. People have a tendency to treat you differently when you have a defect. When other kids were playing on the playground I was left out of their games. If one of their games included a monster, I was asked to play so I could be the monster.

I was glad to be the monster if that meant having somebody to play with...

We were told that football was only for boys and that girls had no business playing football, especially when the girls had to wear dresses or skirts to school. We were not allowed to wear pants to school during those years. I was already a monster, so why not play rough? Football was fun, especially when I got to tackle the boys. Naturally, I tore my dresses and that really irked Mama.

Sometimes I even wore the torn dress to school so I could play football again. Those were the fun times because I was just one of the guys. But in reality, I was a girl who just wanted to play football.

Whenever my brothers and sisters let me play with them, we played store. We used tree seeds and rabbit poop for money. Whoever had the most rabbit poop and seeds was considered the richest kid on the block. I began saving rabbit poop and dreamed of the day when I had so much that it would take me far away from this place where no one would ever hit me again. Over the years, I learned that rabbit poop was just that—rabbit poop. It didn't take me away from there or anywhere else.

At home I wasn't allowed to sleep on a bed because I wasn't

good enough, but the concrete floor was good enough for the kid called nobody. I wondered if the real reason was that my parents had too many kids and there were not enough beds to go around. Or was it another mind game of my mother's? A blanket in the wintertime was considered a luxury…when I wasn't sitting in the woods.

Stealing food was a genuine talent of mine. I stole from wherever I could. My brothers and sisters were allowed to eat first, but I had to watch and then clean up the dishes. If there was anything left, I got to eat; if not—*que sera, sera.* Mama checked every dish, and Lord help you if she found a spot or the dish was not in the place where she thought it should be. If they weren't to her satisfaction she took them out of the cabinet, whether they had been used or not, for me to wash all over again. She threw some of them at me and I cowered in the corner to lessen the blows. She seemed to enjoy this game and laughed her ugly cackle while throwing them at me and then proceeded to kick me. There was evil in that laugh and it made me cringe. She would have been better off to invest in unbreakable dishes. There should have been an Olympic event called "Dish Throwing." Mama would have won the gold medal for that event. No contest.

When I got hurt from one of her games, she told my father that I wasn't behaving and that I had hurt myself trying to get away from her. Did he really believe her? Why didn't he stop her or just leave her? He never came home except to get some clean clothes or a little sleep, but she didn't even let him sleep. Daddy was left with us while Mama would be gone for hours at a time out on the town.

When Daddy had to go back out fishing my sister Marie was in charge. She learned well from Mama how to hit my other brothers and sisters and I. The only good thing was that I could outrun her at times and I didn't have to stand there and take her rampage. We had some serious knockdown, dragout fights at times.

One bright spot I remember was Easter when my dad stayed up most of the night to make bunny rabbit trails near the house. Dad took three sticks and made the rabbit tracks all over, or at least it appeared to be all over the yard. We spent a long time just following the trail, wondering where the rabbit came from. We even got a chocolate Easter bunny and a real Easter basket with grass and candy in it. That is one of the few times I think I really laughed until my belly hurt. That rabbit came just to see me, even for a moment. I called the rabbit Floppy because he just flopped all over the yard with his bunny feet. I never did find the bunny hole. Years later, my dad told me he had placed those tracks there. Thank God for a moment of joy.

School was a place of safety for me, and I wished each day would not end. I knew what was waiting at home and many days I missed the bus on purpose. The walk home had its good moments, especially during the fruit season. Near the house lived a man we called Indian Joe. He lived in a shack at the end of the bend in the road and was known by the townsfolk to be crazy, but he had the best guavas in town. The place was really eerie, but during this time of year we chanced going on the property just to get a few guavas. I never knew what my supper would be that night. Stealing guavas was better than going hungry. If we saw Indian Joe, we waited until he went back into his shack before running up to the vines and snatching the fruit.

One day he caught me and I was so scared I thought I was going to wet my pants. His voice was not gruff like Mama's.

He just asked me why we stole the fruit instead of asking him for it. He held on to my arm and I cried and screamed, "Let me go! You're crazy."

"So that's what they say about me, is it?" he asked. I nodded yes, but couldn't say anything. When I quit squirming, he released his hold on me and we began to talk. He asked my name. *Nobody crazy would ask my name, would they?* I wondered to myself. He told me I could get some guavas, but if I saw him to make sure I spoke to him.

Indian Joe became my friend. I was the one-eyed crazy kid who actually made friends with crazy Indian Joe. Two crazies talking wasn't bad—it was if we understood each other. Did two crazies make a normal? Maybe not, but Indian Joe and I thought so.

The next couple of years were good for Indian Joe and me. I learned a lot about the trees and the Indian tribe he was from. But, I had to be careful, because if Mama ever found out I had a friend she would have made big trouble for me. I wasn't supposed to have any friends. When I was in third grade, Indian Joe died. When no one was looking I cried for him. I didn't find his grave to put some wildflowers on. He would have liked that, I was sure. My heart felt like it would burst every time I passed his little shack in the bend. *Maybe he's happy now,* I told myself; no one could ever call him crazy again. Some of the people in the town burned his shack down. It was as if they didn't want the evil spirits to get their kids if they went there. He wasn't evil or crazy in my book, or in my heart. He was Indian Joe. The others just didn't understand.

Chapter 4

THE HOME FRONT, if you could call it that, was one of uncertainty and hurt. If you wanted to call someone crazy, that was Mama. I began to call her a witch under my breath and wanted to put an evil spell on her to make her into a good witch—or just have her die. The idea was to get rid of the evil, but that wasn't going to happen and somehow I knew that. Her good personality would come in spurts, but the evil was never far behind. You always had to sleep with one eye open and remember to stay out of the way.

Between having to sit in the woods and being awakened at two o'clock in the morning to wash the screens outside, I dreamed of the day I would escape her hands. My dreams were the only safe place for me, besides school—where no one could hurt me. There were nights that, even in my dreams, the hurts surfaced and made sleep an unwelcome friend.

This one day she must have been having a bad-hair day. Her eyes were red with fire when she walked into the house. She began throwing things and screaming. One of the objects hit me in the head and slit the right side of my head open like a banana peel. It was a mustard jar and it splattered all over the grocery boxes and wall. That mustard stain was on the wall for a pretty long time.

Another trip to the emergency room, this time Mama told the doctor that I fell out of the tree in the front yard. That was a stupid excuse, especially when we jumped out of the trees all the time to see who could jump the farthest. Didn't she know you don't get hurt jumping out of trees? You only got hurt when someone threw things at you! I didn't think the doctor believed her. I knew the doctor didn't believe her when the social worker showed up before I got sewed up.

"On the road again," became my motto. The next foster home was pretty much a blur. The only thing I remember was that they didn't hit you, but by now I had learned that if someone wasn't hitting you then you weren't loved. I tried everything I could do to make them hit me, but they never did. I heard the lady tell the social worker that she would have to come get me because I was disrupting the whole family. I kept my clothes in the pillowcase so I wouldn't have to repack the next time I went somewhere.

I was only there for a few weeks when the judge sent me back home. *Those foster parents didn't love me,* I decided—they never once hit me or hurt me. They didn't scream at me when I did bad things in the house. They didn't even scream when I threw a kitten against a wall. I just laughed because I had hurt something and it couldn't hurt me back. So it was back to Mama's I went.

The social worker came every day for the next couple of months to make her report to the judge. The reports to the judge must have said that Mama had changed, but they didn't know Mama. Snakes don't change, they just lie in wait for the next opportunity to strike. The social worker gave her final report to the judge and the judge let me stay in the home. Oh, how little these grown-ups knew about little kids and their feelings.

At school, I had become a little heathen. I loved my third grade teacher, Mrs. Fink. She was the one who had taken care of me when I was younger, but she looked so much older now. When the report cards came out I was given an F in citizen-ship. She had written in cursive on two yellow pieces of paper, front and back. It listed everything I had done during that grading period. I thought I had done so well that there wasn't enough room on the report card to list all the good things I had done. Little did I know they were all the problems I had caused in her classroom. If I could have read cursive I would've thrown that piece of handiwork away before my daddy saw it. An F in citizenship was bad enough, but to have your teacher sharing your "business activities" with your parents?! That was just down right mean, in my mind.

The look on his face told me that the paper was anything but good. I hid in the doghouse because big people couldn't crawl into doghouses. What I didn't know was that big people don't crawl into doghouses—they just push them over. I ran when he pushed it over and he ran after me with a switch. Luckily, I made it around the house twice before he caught up with me. He wore out that switch on my backside until blood ran from my legs and back. It was hard to sit or walk the next week from being so sore. My teacher knew what had happened because I became one of her best students—the quietest the world had ever seen.

The next report card had an A in citizenship, and no yellow sheet of paper with cursive writing went home with me the rest of the year. She was very nice to me the rest of the year, but she was nice to everyone in our class. Did she still remember where I came from and who my mama was? She must have remembered something about me in her heart, though she never mentioned my having stayed with them. It was like a secret place in time that I could not return to because the memories might get stirred up and I'd wish I could go back there to that time again. But I couldn't go back there no matter how much I wanted to.

Mama had begun spending more time away from home and we were left to fend for ourselves. God help you if she came home and found anything missing from the icebox. One day she came home and found a hot dog missing. My little brother had gotten a hot dog out of the icebox, but she said he was too little to have done that. This time she lined all the older kids up to solve this whodunit, *The Mystery of the Missing Hot Dog.* At first, she hit all of us with the belt. Then I admitted eating the hot dog in order to protect the others. She began hitting me with her fist and demanded to know why I had gotten into the icebox. Finally I admitted I ate the hot dog because I was hungry. Then she went wild and began hitting me and kicking me, one for eating the hot dog and the other for lying to her.

Next time, I'm going to eat all the hot dogs in the icebox, with mustard and ketchup, I decided. *I'll even add a can of pork-&-beans to it as well.* It wouldn't have mattered who got the hot dog, she just needed a scapegoat on whom to vent her anger. I began to admit to things I didn't do just to keep the others out of trouble. I no longer could tell the truth from a lie. If anything went wrong in the house there would be trouble and I caught all of it and paid dearly for it. I became the daily object of her wrath, even when nothing went wrong.

When her friends or my brothers' and sisters' friends came over, I wasn't allowed to be seen or heard. I had to become nonexistent. I was sent to the closet in my father's room every time and I sat in there for hours at a time. After awhile I was like a conditioned dog. When company arrived, I immediately went to the closet. That closet became my friend. I can tell you about every piece of wood and every hole in the wall. I could sleep in peace and daydream in peace in that closet. Not even the boogeyman could get me in there.

Grandpa knew I was in the closet and he argued with Mama about it, but that didn't do much good. I knew I would receive the worst of that argument at a later time. Grandpa sometimes came to the closet and sat in there with me and talked to me. As big as a third grader could be, I still tried to sit in my grandfather's lap and snuggle into his chest. I never cried in his lap, especially when I knew that would hurt him. Sometimes I saw tears in his eyes when he held me close. Somehow he knew he couldn't always protect me from what was outside that closet.

The closet became my home for the next couple of years when I wasn't in school, doing Mama's chores, or taking care of the other kids. As I grew older, the closet seemed to get smaller and it was hard to stretch out my legs in there, yet it was still better than the other parts of the house. She could only kick me while I was in there and her fists couldn't harm me. I guess she learned that when she raised her fists to hit me she would end up hitting some other part of the closet. For that I was grateful. The only part of staying in the closet I didn't like was not being able to eat with the rest of the family. There was no one to talk to.

Sure, I got some of the leftovers when it was time to do the dishes, but I had to make sure not to get caught eating them. That just meant the crazy woman would ride again. Instead, I went to school and looked in the garbage cans for parts of lunches the other kids threw away. On good days I found pieces of sandwiches or a potato stick in the garbage. You never really had a feast until you found several garbage can french fries all in the same pack. Most of the kids had peanut butter and jelly sandwiches for lunch so there were plenty of pieces of bread with peanut butter on them. They were really a sight for sore eyes. The only thing was, I had to be careful because the teachers would patrol the area. If I got caught they might have told Mama about my garbage trips and I sure wasn't going to give up my gold mine for anybody.

What I didn't know was that the teachers at school already knew of my gold mine in the cafeteria garbage cans, and I began to be given a lunch at school. Somehow Mama never found out about it and I sure wasn't going to tell her. I didn't even have to pay for it. The teachers at school didn't tell her either. It was as if they were trying to protect me from the mad woman at home. Was it my bruises they saw, or my behavior that made them not tell Mama about the lunches?

Every once in a while the farmers brought watermelon, bell peppers, or other produce to the school for the kids. We all ate until we couldn't put another thing into our bulging bellies. I tried to stuff extra fruit and veggies in my clothes to eat on the way home, knowing I may or may not get to eat when I got home. On those days I walked real slow so I could eat all I wanted.

When we weren't in school, Daddy took us fishing with him. He had his own crew whenever my brothers and sisters helped on the boat. Out on the boat I felt free; free from Mama and free from the hurts and worries of days past as well as the future. The stars lit the midnight sky and shined as if they were talking just to me. I wondered what would happen if I could join them for just a moment. Then the sun appeared over the horizon and the stars began to lose their luster as if even they had their moments in time. God seemed to make them only for a season, and then they too were gone like everything else.

Daddy would be up in the bow of the boat looking over the water. Depending on the time of year we caught different kinds of fish. In the summer we looked for mullet, shiners, and bottom fish. Daddy told us that you could tell how many mullet were in the area by how they skipped across the water. A fat mullet may only skip across the water twice, but a skinny mullet would skip as many as six times. If we saw more than ten mullet skip at a time, Daddy stopped the big boat and we jumped over into the water and held the end of the net while he silently rowed around our catch for the day so as not to disturb the fish. We began pulling the net around in a circle, making the circle smaller and smaller until the fish began to boil in a tiny circle. Most of the time the fish tried to jump over the net and would hit us while trying to escape. Sometimes I felt just like those fish, wanting to escape but with nowhere to go and just caught in the tiny circle of the net.

Oops! Wrong Family

Some just gave up trying because the fight in them was gone. Where was my fight to survive? Or was I getting good at just staying alive?

In the wintertime we fished for mackerel, blue fish, and bass. Daddy said you could smell the mackerel. He was right, they sure did stink. They had a silver streak that shimmered in the water. I really identified with the mackerel because my life stank, too, but unlike them I couldn't just swim away. I was just a stinkpot in my mama's heart and mind from the start.

Any chance I got to work at the fish house was a blessing for me, even when my parents took the money I earned to help pay for my clothes. I worked hard at the fish house, thinking one day it would be my way out. But it wasn't. When I got home Mama beat me because I smelled like fish. Why not—when you work with the fish, you smell like the fish. It was a really good week when I didn't get hit for three days in a row, and there actually were a few times like that.

The day came when I knew my father wasn't coming back. Mama had thrown all his clothes out on the back step. I remember that day because my dad had a turtle on the back step. The turtle was going to be our dinner that night, but dinner wasn't to be. The electric man was there to get the money for the electricity we used up.

It was funny how all my brothers and sisters cried, but I was the only one who could not cry. All my tears had been spent long before. I was angry at my dad for leaving because he was now free and I was still a prisoner. No, it wasn't a home. It was a house of horrors that no one should ever have had to live in. Now Mama had free reign to do whatever she wanted and the abuse stepped up a notch.

She had this awful laugh as she played her games. That laugh alone was evidence enough to let you know she had something else in store.

One of the things my brothers and sisters and I liked to do was dig deep holes in the dirt. We got to where we could dig down over our heads and connect other holes in the dirt and make a tunnel. The Vietnam War was raging and we built tunnels in the dirt to save our family if the war came to our house. Sometimes we dug a hole and covered each other up to our necks. One of the tunnels caved in on my little brother one day and we had to dig him out. We screamed a lot as we dug as fast as we could to get him out. It seemed like hours, but it was only a few minutes before we got him unstuck. We only dug short tunnels after that.

I wasn't even allowed to get sick like normal kids. When the other kids were sick and throwing up, it was my job not only to clean up their mess but also to stay home and take care of them. If it wasn't to Mama's satisfaction she had another one of her fits. If I got sick I got the fullness of her wrath, so I learned not to be sick. It got to the point where I couldn't tell if I was sick or not. For every cough there was a hit across the head.

Some days she became scarier than others. She had this gun you could put bullets in and then spin the chamber. She often took one bullet and put it in the chamber and spun the barrel. Then she pointed it at my head and started laughing, saying "See this gun? I'm going to kill you like I'm going to kill your father." Then she pointed the gun at my head and pulled the trigger. I used to wish that the bullet would come out, but it never did. It would have been better for me if I was dead. Then Mama couldn't play her games anymore and I wouldn't be hurt ever again.

This went on for the next couple of years until she lost the gun. I never found out where it went. I bet Grandpa found out what was happening and took it away from her. If not, then I'm glad it got lost.

Chapter 5

WHEN I STARTED junior high, things weren't much better. We had moved to Palm Beach, Florida and she was there to make a name for herself—and did she ever! She worked as a bar maid and we kids were on our own many nights. That was just fine with me until she began bringing men home with her and we became her little prostitutes. Only my older sister and I were used in this sick game. My sister got the worst of it because she was older and more mature looking. God help us if we ever told anyone because Mama's money source would have been cut off. She even went so far as to answer the door naked when the men came over.

Mama took us to church, but she always had an ulterior motive. It was to see how much she could get out of the church. She said things like, "I need food for my starving children," and got food and money from the people at the church. I often hid under the pews at the church because of my shame of being in this family—either that or sheer embarrassment, I'm still not sure which.

She really was the queen of con. She gave new meaning to the word *hypocrite*. She was an expert at using people and then throwing them away after their usefulness was gone. Heaven help you if she found out you had money and were a very sympathetic person. I'm sure some people must have found out about her little game, but she was so good at it. During those times, I felt ashamed of how she could manipulate people in to doing things for her in the name of the children. It seemed as if we were nothing but pawns in her sight.

At church, we were told that God was like our parents. If that was so, I didn't want any part of God. That meant He was one who hurt you, then threw you away just like Mama did.

There were two people who weren't fooled by her, my Uncle Joe and Aunt Ruth. They used to give her money for us, but the money was always used for her own personal needs and pleasures. My uncle started bringing food instead. We were able to have Christmas several times because of what my aunt and uncle brought. One Christmas, I got a bicycle and it was worth a million dollars in my book. Mama ran them off after a few Christmases, especially since she knew her money flow had been cut off and she couldn't use them anymore for her own shenanigans.

I loved seeing my aunt and uncle because they always showed us kindness and she always smelled so good. I dreamed of the day that I could be like my aunt and uncle. I didn't know how or why they showed such kindness. Later in life, I discovered that it was called love and perfume. My aunt and uncle were my heroes and they still are to this day. They loved God with all their hearts and showed such a different side of God then my mama did. I truly wished they were my mom and dad. I once even told them I was in the wrong family.

One night, Mama came home hurt from her job at the bar. It was my turn to laugh, but she was not to see what was on my heart. I wished she was dead—then I wouldn't hurt anymore. She had fallen off a barstool at work and her knee swelled up. She hobbled over to a chair in the kitchen and sat down. She made me rub her knee and hold ice on it for a long time. I must not have done it right because she hit me over the head with her fist. When I tried to move away from her she screamed for me to get back over by the chair. You didn't disobey her, even when you knew the trouble awaiting you.

One of the most ridiculous things she ever did was when she thought she was Lady Godiva. She rode down main street naked, on a horse, with her long, blonde hair flowing in the wind. It must have been quite a sight for the community. The next day at school I had more fights than you could imagine, especially when the kids called me "Little Godiva." Mama seemed to thrive on her eccentric and attention-getting behavior. Because of her actions we were called the crazy kids.

The neighbors were afraid of the crazy woman and her children. At night, we rode our bicycles up and down the streets carrying lighted newspapers for torches in order to see. The people in the neighborhood thought we were going to burn their houses down. Boy, grown-ups sure did think differently than kids. We might have been crazy, but we weren't dangerous.

Oops! Wrong Family

One day the police came to the house and began throwing all our belongings and furniture on the street. Little did I know that we were being evicted. We must have done a lot of bad because the police escorted us over the bridge and we were told never to come back. Mama sure was mad that day.

There were so many of us that I always had to ride in the trunk of the car with a couple other brothers and sisters. Mama told me I wasn't good enough to see people, but we kids made a game out of being in the trunk. The trunk lid was tied down just enough to let some air in and we peeked through the opening to see the cars go by. We were very bold on some days and stuck out our fingers and pretend they were chicken feathers. People just stared at the trunk as they went by and pointed either at us or our mother. Thank God Mama never found out about that game. I wondered if she knew why people were shaking their fingers at her.

After a couple of months, Mama dropped us off at the courthouse with all our clothes. She was not able to take care of us because it cramped her lifestyle and the man she was living with. At that man's house, he made us eat eggshells with a lot of bread because he said it was healthy for us.

This time there was no respecter of persons. (See Acts 10:34, KJV.) We were dropped off on the courthouse steps, with our clothes in the pillowcases that held them. My older sister stayed in the car. My mother said something about it being all my fault and then just drove away. By now, I had realized that not everything could be my fault.

I went into the courthouse and told them my brothers and sisters were out on the steps and had nowhere to go. At thirteen-years-old I had become the spokesman for my family. The people at the court took us over to some lady's house with a fence around it. We stayed there for the next couple of months and took all kinds of psychiatric tests. Did they think I was crazy? Or did they think our family was crazy? It was from one of these tests that I learned my IQ was 127. Go figure…

While there, we were not allowed outside the fence or to go to school. The toys in the yard were not for our age group, but we played with them anyway. If we went outside the gate the lady told us we would end up on Forty-fifth Street. That was the place where all the bad kids went and you sure didn't want to go there. I heard that once you went there you never got out until you died. And I wasn't ready to die, not just yet. When I found out that my older sister was on Forty-fifth Street, I wanted to go there because there was nothing worse than being alone and feeling no one cared about you. When I told the foster parent I wanted to go, she said that the courts were trying to find a place for all of us to go and my sister would have a place to go, too.

There was a boy in that home and we got caught in bed together. He said he loved me and wanted to prove he loved me. I thought that was what you were supposed to do to find love. Hadn't my real mother taught us that when those old men touched us? It didn't seem abnormal to be in bed with this boy. The things you experience every day become normal until you are shown something different. What was so different about this situation from the situation at home? I got into a lot of trouble over that and I thought about running away, but I couldn't. I had to protect the others from getting hurt.

Where I came from, everyone was an enemy—no one was your friend, especially the social workers. They told you where to go, when to sit, and what to do. I had become so conditioned that no one got within arm's length of me. That meant they could hurt me and my head could become a bowling ball at any moment. I vowed no one would ever hurt me again. If anyone got too close I just started shaking and crying, and then I ran away from them. I even walked out on the teachers at school when they got too close. I always looked for an escape route.

The social workers must have called some of our relatives because my aunt and uncle and several others came. Our family was split up between several relatives' homes. I wanted to stay with my aunt and uncle because they were my heroes, but my younger brother and sister got to stay with them. I stayed with my uncle until my dad came down.

I still believed you weren't loved if you weren't being beat. The foster parents I had had never hit me, so naturally I believed they didn't love me. I did all sorts of things to make them angry, but they always held their tongues and fists. One time, I even sat on their oven door to break it, but the foster father just swatted me one time on the butt. That meant I was loved, or so I believed.

Chapter 6

Uncle Joe and Aunt Ruth lived on a farm and took their kids and me to church every Sunday. I still felt like an outcast and unloved, even at church. When things went wrong at the house, I always admitted to the wrongdoing out of habit, knowing I would be punished. To my mind, that meant they loved me.

One day, one of the other kids did something and I admitted to it, much to my chagrin. Uncle Joe took off his belt and hit the refrigerator door so hard that it knocked the paint off. He said to me, "If you ever admit to something you didn't do, I'll tear you up like this refrigerator." That was the beginning of my learning a whole new way of living. I didn't know that way of life then. I am very grateful to him for that lesson.

We ended up going to court for my parent's divorce. There

were a lot of people in the courtroom, but we had to stay outside until the judge called us in to testify about our home life. You had to be at least twelve years old before the judge would let you choose which parent you wished to live with. The judge asked a lot of questions. One question he asked was, "How did your mother answer the door?" I told them she answered the door buck naked. One of the fishermen in the courtroom shouted, "You tell 'em honey," which caused a lot of laughter. I was embarrassed. The judge then asked, "What would you do if you had to go live with your mother?" I told the judge I would run away. I couldn't even look at my mother because I knew I would be dead if I had to go back with her now.

When we were led out of the courtroom, we stood down by the bottom of the stairs ready to run if we had to go back to her. Taking whatever came from the outside world was better than ever facing home again.

The verdict came and custody of all the kids was awarded to my father, except for my older sister who chose to live with Mama. Why not, she was my mother's pick of the family, anyway. It seemed like we were in heaven when my father told us we would be living with him. What I didn't know at the time was that my physical education teacher and her husband, Mr. and Mrs. Sigurdson, had gone to the judge on my behalf and asked the judge if they could adopt me. They didn't adopt me, but I was still adopted in their hearts.

The time came when we all had to go live with my dad and stepmother. She was twenty-three-years-old and I was now thirteen. I thought it was going to be better, but it was the beginning of another type of abuse. But this time, it came from my stepmother. We became the tyrants of the home. My stepmother was there because she loved my dad. I didn't know a twenty-three-year-old had no concept of, or experience with, how to deal with seven inherited kids and all of their psychological hang ups.

Chores and babysitting were a daily ordeal. When they weren't done right I got hit for it, but not as bad as with Mama. Mama made a lot of trouble for my dad and stepmom. She cursed at them and tried to physically remove some of the other kids from the yard, knowing a fight would be the result of her actions.

One day, Mama was running after my little brother. I didn't know if she was going to hurt him or not, but I'd had enough. I caught up with her and just when she turned around I punched her with all my might. Boy did she hit the ground hard! When she looked up I told her, "If you ever hit one of us again, I'll blow you away." If I'd had a machine gun at that moment I probably would have blown her to pieces right there in the yard.

Food was scarce again, and if you didn't get home from school in time for dinner, all the food would be gone. The adults and smaller children ate first, then the older kids got to eat. By the time I got my chance, the food had all been gobbled up; however, I still had to do the dishes. Working at the fish house helped because they often fried fish for the workers to eat. I ate so many it's a wonder I didn't grow gills.

Mama came to school and got me out of class just to yell at me and let me know all the trouble she was having was my fault. I wouldn't walk on the sidewalk with her. She told me to get beside her and that I was embarrassing her. I'd rather have been in trouble for walking on the grass than walking beside her.

When Mama came to the school, my physical education

teacher stood in the door of the gym and made sure she didn't hurt me. Mrs. Sigurdson told me to never shut the car door when I was with Mama so I could jump out of the car and run if she went to hit me. Mrs. Sigurdson became my protector from Mama. I wished she was my mother. She gave me passes to my next class so I wouldn't be in trouble with my English teacher.

I always thought it was kind of funny when someone got caught chewing gum in her class. Mrs. Sigurdson made that student dig a grave for their gum in front of the class and put a little cross on it. We had our own gum cemetery at the school.

Mrs. Sigurdson got transferred over to the high school when I was in eighth grade and the principal over there told her not to have anything to do with me. When she told me that, I felt like I had no reason for living. I became numb. Nothing in my life mattered any longer. That high school principal didn't have a clue what her statement did to me. There is an old saying, "Sticks and stones will break my bones, but words will never hurt me." But words matter, and they do hurt, especially when they come from someone who can take your very lifeline away from you. For a kid that was a nobody, Mrs. Sigurdson made me feel like a somebody. I took a whole bottle of aspirin and nonchalantly told Mrs. Sigurdson. I don't think she believed me. Why would she? I didn't even die. How was I to know God was watching over me?

Thank God for my principal at the junior high school. He must have gotten wind of what was said, especially because he told her, "We are going to lose this kid if you don't keep contact with her." That's when Mrs. Sigurdson started coming to school on certain days to pick me up. The principal at the junior high always called me to the office to let me know when she was coming.

It was a while before I began to talk to her about my past. When she asked about my home I just went silent. She dropped me off at the trail in the woods that led to my house because my parents thought she was a troublemaker. All I knew was that I felt safe as long as I could see her from a distance or say a couple of words to her. She never found out that I rode a bus from the junior high to the high school just to say hi to her, then jumped back on the bus to ride home. There were times I missed the bus and had to walk home. I knew there would be a beating for missing the bus and not being home on time, but it didn't matter.

I found out when Mrs. Sigurdson's birthday was and I had somehow managed to save twenty dollars for a present for her. As usual, I took the school bus over to the high school and told her happy birthday and handed her an envelope with the money in it. When she opened it she told me she couldn't take it and gave it back to me. I literally begged her to keep it, and a pick-up-and-toss game went back and forth. She told me to leave so I wouldn't miss the bus. In tears, I took the twenty dollars and threw it into a trash can. If she didn't want it, I didn't want it either. I didn't know at the time that teachers could not take gifts from their students. Her family later became a significant part of my life, and I am grateful to them.

Once, when I was in ninth grade, I had an eye appointment that was in a town far from where we lived. It just so happened that Mr. and Mrs. Sigurdson lived in that town and for some reason my parents let them take me to the doctor's office and let me spend the night at their house. My parents came and got me the next day. That was almost forty years ago, but that day stuck in my memory as a huge milestone in seeing that what I had at home wasn't what I wanted it to be. That night I had my own bed to sleep in, alone, with two covers, not just one or a piece of one. Mrs. Sigurdson covered me up and they both told me to sleep well. *Why were they so soft-spoken and gentle?* I wondered. I thought my aunt and uncle were the only ones that way, but there seemed to be other people in the world who cared about other peoples' hurts, too. Maybe they really didn't know my world and they were just being themselves.

The next morning they gently woke me up. I knew I was either in the wrong house or in heaven. To find out which, I played possum in that fine bed with two covers to see if they would come back in again. To my utter amazement they did, and gently called my name again and said breakfast was ready. I smelled bacon. At home we ate corn flakes and Cheerios for breakfast. They had Raisin Bran and bacon on the table. Mr. Sigurdson poured a glass of milk and put it in front of me. I took the glass of milk and poured it on the cereal. They looked at me a little puzzled as if to say, "What in the world are you doing, child?" I told him I wasn't allowed to have milk in a glass, but instead of getting mad he just filled the glass with milk again and let me know I could have more if I wanted. I sure must have looked funny to them as this big, fourteen-year-old kid just sat there and cried. To be honest, I didn't know what to say or feel. I just sat there and cried, wishing they were my parents.

It would be a long time before I saw a glass of milk by itself again. That glass of milk was worth more than a million bucks to me. I thought they were rich and yet there was something different about them. They cared about *me*.

When my father came to pick me up the next day I did not want to go home. I cried half the way home. As my father drove off, I kept my eyes glued to them because I thought I would never see them again. But over the years, our paths crossed again and again.

That ride home seemed like an eternity. I had seen a home that was so different from mine. I just couldn't put it into words. Now I know it was a thing called unconditional love that came from their relationship with Jesus. They didn't care that I looked ugly with my blind eye, that my clothes were held together by safety pins, or that I felt like the bottom of a dung pile. When I spoke I couldn't look them in the eye for fear they wouldn't accept me if they saw the real me. But all they saw was a kid that needed their help, and they met that need.

The next couple years were a blur. I felt I had never existed to anyone or anything. Sometimes my mind played funny little tricks on me in order to keep my sanity. People often have, buried deep within themselves, hurts and memories so harsh that to bring them up would seem unreal to the world around them. As a result, they learn to survive and function without really living.

The time was growing near for me to leave home. It was unbearable at home, with the blame for everything going wrong constantly aimed at me. My father came in one morning in a rage and began hitting me and yelling that it was all my fault that my stepmother and he were having problems and that she may be leaving. I didn't have any clue what he was talking about. I would have been better off in any other family than the situation in which I found myself at that moment. After he left the room, I vowed to leave that place. It would be just a matter of time.

Chapter 7

I BEGAN TAKING MONEY out of my paycheck every week before handing it over to my stepmother. My dad and stepmother told me I had to help pay for the family. Family? All I saw was a bunch of raggedy kids—and I was one of 'em. During this period, I was careful not to take too much out of my paycheck so my stepmother would not get suspicious. I mailed the money to a friend in Long Island, New York and she put it into a savings account for me. It grew to nearly six hundred dollars before I split that house for good. I vowed I would never return, and that if I ever had a family it wouldn't be like this one. At that time I didn't know what I wanted, but I knew it wasn't like that place.

The day to leave and venture out on my own came sooner than I had planned. My stepmother came to the fish house and told me I had to go home and watch the kids. I told her I had to finish work first. For some reason that was the wrong answer. She got angry and yelled, "Don't make me make a scene right here!" Then she raised her hand to hit me, but I ducked. If she had connected, there would have been blood—not on her hand, but on my face. This really made her mad and she came over and repeatedly hit me over the head while all the fishermen watched. She left in a huff. I crouched down on my knees sobbing from the rage and humiliation I felt in front of my coworkers. I knew at that moment that if I was ever to be safe I had to leave right then.

When I got home I informed my dad and stepmother that I was leaving. I ran out of the house and hid under the kitchen window only to hear them arguing in the kitchen.

"You can't let her go, she's crazy!" exclaimed my stepmother. My father responded, "Just let her go. She'll be back."

That night I slept in the woods. The next day I found a one-room trailer to rent and I never went back to their house. The trailer was awfully small, but it did keep the rain off my head and I was now making my own decisions. I thought I was all grown up. I thought I was free. Oh, how wrong I was, as I would find out in the years to come.

Being out on your own, alone, does not always mean freedom. Now the choices I made would bring either doubt and heartache, or laughter and a sense of pride. No one taught me how to live in an uncaring world, but I did know how to survive.

Somehow, I finished high school while working at the fish house after school. Sometimes I stunk just like the fish I worked with. The kids at school made fun of my clothes and the leftover fish smell, even though I showered and scrubbed my skin until I thought it would fall off the bone. Life was difficult, but I vowed I would not be like my family. I cried a lot when I was by myself, too. I didn't know if it was out of self-pity or because I was a nobody that nobody wanted. I felt all alone and could not tell anybody.

My first car was a white Ford Galaxy 500 convertible. It was the prettiest thing I'd ever seen. Now I had something I loved, but there's a funny thing you realize about inanimate objects—they can't love you back. One night, after working at the fish house, I was driving along at seventy-five miles per hour on my way to the home of the foster parents I had at that time. In 1970, seventy-five was considered fast. When I saw blue lights in my rearview mirror, I pulled over. The officer asked me where I was going in such a hurry, but then backed away from the door of the car. He asked what the smell was and must have thought I had something or someone dead in my car from the look on his face. I told him that I had just gotten off work at the local fish house and was on my way to my foster parent's home to get a bath. He let me go without giving me a ticket, and I was grateful for a small favor.

I went out to visit my foster mother at least three or four times a week because she was kind to me. I held on to any ounce of kindness from anyone. These trips didn't last long due to their divorce the next year. My foster mom remarried, but I wasn't allowed to visit. Between the smell of fish and the uncertainty of my behavior, I felt as if she threw me away, too. I cried so much that I probably could have taken a bath in a tub filled with all the tears. Within the following year, I found out that my foster mother had died. She and her new husband were killed in a car accident. I didn't go to the funeral due to my finding out well after their deaths.

Oops! Wrong Family

When I graduated from high school I got a scholarship for $250 to Indian River Community College. The man who interviewed me either felt sorry for me or gave me the scholarship when I offered to bring him some number twelve fishing twine. I kept my word and brought him the twine as I promised. My dad always said, "If your word is no good, neither is the paper you sign." For some reason, the man and his wife took an interest in me and kept up with me for a long while. I was able to finish my first semester at the college. The courses seemed pretty hard at the time. Math was my worst subject and I barely passed.

You had to pay your next semester's tuition before it started. I owed money and had about ten days to get it. I worked to get the money and had three different checks to hand them to pay the bill. It meant I couldn't buy food that week, but I could go to school the next semester. The drive to not be like my family was worth being hungry for a short while. Besides, the garbage cans always had some left over french fries or pieces of sandwich in them. I vowed that when I got out of school I would never eat garbage can food and never go hungry again. Little did I know that when I brought the three checks to the cashier, someone had already paid my tuition. I asked several times because I had the money to pay the bill, and I certainly had not paid it already.

I did not return to that college after the following semester because the owner of the fish house asked me to manage the restaurant in West Palm Beach, Florida. Naturally, I moved there, not only to get away from my family, but also to get away from my life. Funny thing was, I tried to get away from my life but ended up carrying it with me—all the problems, emotional hurts, and scars became excess baggage.

I found a school there, but I had to work to pay for tuition and books. Now I had the choice of working and paying for an apartment, or living in my car and going to school. Living in my car was not forever, I thought, and if I got my education I would not be like my family. The irony was that the school in which I enrolled was connected to the church my mother had conned years earlier. That memory brought back a lot of shame and guilt, and I wondered if the people at the college and church thought I was going to be like my mother. Every time they looked at me funny, I swore I knew what they were thinking.

Classes began and my Galaxy 500 was holding up well. I still smelled like fish at times, and very few people would even give me the time of day. The dean of women at the college became my only means of feeling human, but even that was taxing on a person. It was as if the more I went to her office, the more she dreaded my even showing up. After a while, she either closed her door or said she was too busy. I guess I just wore out my welcome.

The church across the street was affiliated with the college and there were people there, but no real God, so I thought. One family, Roger and Tobie Stitt, took me under their wing and trusted me to babysit their kids in order to help me make ends meet. Over the next couple of years they helped me in small but profound ways. Any act of kindness was big in my book. When Christmas came, they gave me a present. All I could do was cry because I could not give back to them. I couldn't even open the present because I thought it too valuable to receive. *Why would anyone want to give me something?* I wondered.

During this time, my defenses began to come down a little.

Oops! Wrong Family

Roger and Tobie let me stay the night at their home when I watched their kids. There were many times they paid me more than I had earned. Tobie taught me how to crochet and boy did that come in handy a couple years later when I went to school in West Virginia. I often thought that if there was a Mr. and Mrs. Angel Award, they would have gotten it. Our paths crossed several more times over the next few years.

When my defenses started to come down, I became an emotional wreck. Everything I believed and thought was normal was not the norm at all. I had to change my thinking and ways—but to what? I hit bottom and tried suicide as a means of escape. Everything in my life stunk: my job, my living situation, my relationships, and my thoughts. It was overwhelming. What was I to do? I still lived in my car, took showers at the fish house, and I had a loaf of bread and a jar of peanut butter to survive on for two weeks. After six months of this type of "living," I found myself with no money to buy bread or even a jar of peanut butter.

I remembered my aunt and uncle, so I borrowed a dime and called them collect. I asked them if I could borrow two dollars to buy bread and peanut butter so I could eat and be able to go to school. My aunt got upset with me because I hadn't let her know about the situation I was in. What made this more ridiculous from their point of view was that they owned a grocery store at the time and their niece was afraid to ask for food. My aunt sent me a bus ticket and I went down to their home in Pompano, Florida.

When I arrived, my aunt hugged me and made comments like, "For the life of me, child, why didn't you call before now?" I never saw so much food as when I visited them. I ate very little because I thought it would run out and we needed to save it for the next day. My aunt could not understand my thinking at all. There was different food on the table the next day and the next couple of days after that. I even got to sleep in my own bed in a separate room. That was like heaven to me, especially after sleeping in the car for so long. When they took me back to the college, my car's trunk was packed so full of food that I thought I had died and gone to heaven!

My aunt also took me shopping and bought me new clothes. The new clothes were a far cry from what I had on at the time, and they smelled good, too. She seemed like a millionaire to me. She loved me unconditionally and didn't want any of the clothes back after I wore them. These were the first new clothes I had seen in a while, and there was no angle to her giving. During the next few years I visited my aunt and uncle often, even though I was still afraid of people at times.

My irrational thinking slowly was being changed, especially when I heard my aunt praying at night. I never told my aunt what was in my heart, but somehow she knew. When she prayed, it was as if something or someone was spying on me and spilling the beans, so to speak, because my secret thoughts seemed to come out of her mouth. How did she know? Her prayers stayed in my mind for a long time after I left. My heart was slowly becoming human and the hardness in it was being chipped away. I still thought mushy hearts set you up for hurt, but I was becoming a little more willing to trust.

My aunt made a way for me to get into the dorm, but I still had to furnish my own food because I didn't have the money to buy a lunch ticket. Thank God my aunt and uncle supplied food on a regular basis, too. My roommate at the time was in the same situation so we shared what we had. This was the first give-and-take relationship I had ever known.

Oops! Wrong Family

My roommate was from Panama. She introduced me to the Ouji board and other witchcraft-type activities. We got together several times a week until, one night, we got scared out of our wits. Things in the room started moving without anyone saying or doing anything to make them move. It was freaky.

I began to cut myself every once in a while to get rid of some of my emotional pain. *Why not?* I reasoned; *Maybe some of the emotional pain will leave, too.* Physical pain lasted only a short while, whereas emotional pain lasted a long time. I learned later that emotional pain can only be healed through forgiveness.

Chapter 8

A FEW YEARS LATER I met the man of my dreams. He was six-foot-three inches tall, handsome, and had a smile that could melt any woman's heart. I thought he was a commercial fisherman because he had a net in his boat and lived by the water. Only problem with that theory was that he never mended the holes in his net. Real commercial fishermen took care of their nets because that is how they made a living and fed their families. The holes in his net were so big that a cow could walk through them without getting tangled up. A person would lose a lot of fish through a hole that big. I still believed he was a commercial fisherman, but I soon find out the truth. All I knew then was that I was going to marry him, and marry him I did.

He could sweep you off your feet. He was a good provider

and we lived on the river in a nice home. I could sit on the dock for hours and just watch the boats on the river go back and forth, or see a mullet skip on top of the water. I still hurt inside, however, and didn't know why. Nothing seemed to get rid of the hurt, so I learned to use it as an excuse whenever I was challenged to do better.

We had a daughter and she was beautiful. All parents think their baby is beautiful. We named her Mary Jacquelyn, but we called her Jackie. She was the only girl in a long line of boys on my husband's side of the family. Naturally, she was spoiled by everyone but me. I didn't know how to be a parent. Little by little, I began to understand that this little person had needs, but I didn't know how to meet her needs for love, trust, security, or even comfort. These words were foreign to me. You cannot give away what you have never learned yourself. If you were never loved or comforted, how can you know how to give either of them? If you learned fear of everyone and everything, how would you be able to teach someone to trust? I thought the answer was obvious—you can't.

My husband could still charm any woman with his smile and money. One night he showed up at our door at three in the morning. I grabbed a weapon because I thought he was a burglar. The only thing that saved him was when he yelled, "It's me! It's me! Let me in." Regardless of his flaws, he never physically abused me, nor did he ever tell me I was a nobody. For that I was, and still am, thankful. The only thing I really didn't like was being put on such a tight budget: however, it was better than what I already had been through.

I was beginning to feel like a failure in everything I did. I became a victim of my own abuse. Nobody else was abusing me now, not even my husband—so, why was I still feeling like a nobody that no one wanted? The feelings of worthlessness and inadequacy from my childhood still played havoc with my mind and emotions. Didn't I have everything I wanted? I was married, even though he had other women. I had a child that everyone loved. I wasn't eating out of garbage cans or subsisting on one jar of peanut butter for two weeks at a time. I sure wasn't living in my car. Where was all of this emotional turmoil coming from? I wanted things beyond my grasp, almost as if I was always seeing and never receiving. I always felt empty, but I didn't know how to fill the void. Surely there was something out there to take away the pain and loneliness I felt almost every day of my life.

After my husband and I divorced, he continued to provide financially for the family, and for that I was grateful. He visited because of our daughter, and he was a good daddy by society's standards. At that time, I was in school to become a licensed practical nurse. It was the quickest route for me to get an education and support myself. It was not because I loved to take care of people. I could hardly take care of myself. What does a messed up twenty-two-year-old know about life, anyway?

Before our divorce, I found out that my mother had been pursuing my husband for her own selfish motivations, so I went to her house and confronted her. She denied it and told me she was going to call the police. She stepped away from the front door for a moment and returned with a shotgun. She pointed the weapon at my face, told me she would kill me, and repeated that she was going to call the police if I didn't leave. I offered her the dime to call them, and then I left. I haven't seen her since. Maybe she changed her ways. I hope so!

I had scheduled a vacation for about the same time that my ex-husband was coming for a visit. Jackie and I were scheduled to leave for Long Island, New York, before he arrived. My ex-husband's grandmother told me that if I left before he saw the baby, I would regret it for the rest of my life. On the way home from New York, Jackie was killed in a car accident when my car hit a bridge in St. Augustine, Florida, and flipped five times. She was only eighteen months old. I begged the ambulance attendants to let me hold her one more time, but they whisked her away in another ambulance. Jackie died three hours later and I was never allowed to say good-bye.

At that point, everything I cared about had been taken away from me. My life became unbearable. I had sixteen broken bones, multiple gashes in my face and body, and a compound fracture of my leg. I was patched back together, with rods in my leg and screws in my ankle and hip, but the doctors said I would never walk again. The engine of my car had pushed my hip and right side of my body up two inches, so if I ever did walk I'd look like a penguin waddling along the ice. They also said I would never be a nurse. A couple of years later I was running—and I had become a nurse.

If anyone ever tells you a person in a coma cannot hear what others around them say, tell them they are sorely mistaken. My doctors kept telling everyone I was going to die—but I kept trying to tell them I wasn't dying. They didn't want to tell me Jackie was dead, but I had already heard them tell the staff in the intensive care unit.

When I came around, the nurses were very excited. I told them, "You keep saying I'm going to die, but before I do, can I make one last phone call?" Can you imagine wanting to make your last phone call at three in the morning? One of my foster mothers accepted the collect call. She came up the next morning and arranged transportation to the hospital in Stuart,

Florida. I told her that if I was going to die, I wanted to die at home. The hospital sent the Singing Cowboy, an EMT who carried his guitar with him. He sang most of the way there just to keep me calm. The doctor also gave me a big shot before leaving the hospital to ease the pain. Riding in the ambulance was no picnic.

I wanted to know where God was when it hurt so bad that even my own life seemed like nothing. I cursed at God for a long time after I came out of my coma. I even saved my daily doses of pills for several days and then took them all at once in a feeble attempt at suicide. I was unresponsive for a while, and the nurses were alarmed. I must have spilled the beans because they made sure I didn't poison myself with an overdose. I wasn't too good at hiding my medicine in my cheek, so I spit it out later. All I knew was that Jackie was dead and I felt that my life should have been taken instead of hers. After that, the nurses no longer trusted me taking pills.

After two months in the hospital in Stuart, I was allowed to go home. My aunt and uncle let me stay with them for a while. Their home was the most beautiful I had ever seen. I still wished they were my parents. Here I learned to really like cheese because it seemed my uncle ate cheese with everything. They were rich in my book because they could afford cheese. Some way to think, isn't it? Then came the day when my aunt said it was time for me to go home.

I walked on crutches and crawled from room to room when I didn't have my crutches. For the next twelve years I limped severely without a built-up shoe to compensate for my injured hip. Bitterness and hate invaded the very depths of my soul. Now added to the long string of emotional and physical hurts was the fact that my daughter was dead and I walked funny.

Oops! Wrong Family

While in the hospital I met a nurse named Hilda. Her kindness touched me. I couldn't understand the peace she had. It was if her acts of kindness came from an angel. Whenever I couldn't be handled in the hospital room, they sent Hilda in to talk to me. Sometimes she just sang and a peace came into the room that was indescribable. She asked me to visit her after I was released from the hospital. I wanted to see what made this lady tick.

When I was able to get out to my car on crutches, I drove to Hobe Sound, Florida to visit Hilda. It was a pretty big surprise and I sure wasn't ready for what I was about to discover. The people there dressed strangely, according to my little world. All of the women had their hair up in buns and wore below-the-knee-length dresses with no makeup. The men were dressed in long sleeve shirts and long pants. You never saw them in shorts. They even went swimming in their clothes. That seemed weird, to me. Didn't they know that the weight of their clothes would pull them underwater and they would drown?

They talked about their love for God and practiced what they preached. There was a love about them that I did not understand. They hugged each other and showed genuine concern for one another. They even hugged others who were not their family as if they were part of the family. That seemed so strange to me.

After I arrived there, I met the Newton family. They sort of adopted me along with some of the students who attended a school near their home. Mrs. Newton was beautiful, and when she laughed her whole body gently shook. What I liked most about her laugh was the twinkle in her eye that came with it. Sometimes I would do something on purpose just to watch her laugh, then she would say, "Now Debi…" She seemed to love each student unconditionally, no matter what they did or told her. She was not even afraid to give you a great big hug. If ever there were angels to an abused messed-up nobody, she and Mr. Newton were them.

I believed that nothing was real and nobody kept their word. I always heard that your word was your bond. Did Mrs. Newton really keep her word when she told me she loved me, or was it just another con to break up my only remaining thread of sanity? When she told me she loved me, all I could say was, "Right!" She could not understand why I wasn't able to accept her words as true, but she kept on telling me anyway as if by osmosis I would eventually believe her. When she came close, I just cowered in a corner with my defenses raised wishing her to stay away while at the same time wanting her to hug me like the rest. More than once I broke out in a cold sweat when someone came close just to hug me. Little by little the defenses came down as that family tried to love me back to life.

Mr. Newton looked skinny, but his face lit up when he laughed. His face was always shiny, I guess because he was always happy. Nobody could possibly be that happy—or could they?

He was a missionary pilot and flew missionaries to the Bahamas, so I had the privilege of meeting many of the missionaries when they stayed at the Newton's home. He was the most long-winded preacher I had ever listened to, but I didn't mind because when I was in his presence he made me feel like I was worth something. He would come up to where I was sitting in church and say, "And these women in their pants and short hair," then smile and look at me. You knew you were in for it if he stepped down from the platform where the men preached.

Over time, I could tell them just about anything and they either gave me advice or just shook their heads, but they loved me unconditionally. I began to realize that some of my past hurts and emotionally damaged inner walls were beginning to melt even more. I was becoming an actual person in their eyes. In fact, I was already a special person in their lives—I just didn't know it yet. You never really know what is in the hearts or minds of other people. I felt as if I couldn't measure up to their standards, and God sure wasn't interested in me and my messed up world. Yet there was something different about these people that drew me like a magnet to whatever it was they had. Everyone needs special people in their lives to help them grow and become somebody.

I decided I was going to be like them. We had a pants-cutting party and a lady in the church transformed all my pants into skirts. The women of that church had a ball taking out the seams of this heathen's pants and turned them into skirts of fashion. I looked so funny in those skirts. Some had stripes, some were plaid, and some were plain. They were uncomfortable to sit in and hard to walk or run in. I was still lost, not only to my inner self, but also to God.

One day I went to Mrs. Newton and told her I was going to join the army, but it didn't go over very well. The first thing Mrs. Newton asked me was, "What will you do when you have to do work requiring pants?" I told her I would just wear pants, and I could almost hear her infamous, "Now Debi…" The army recruiters gave me a battery of aptitude tests, the results of which enabled me to pick any field I wanted. But due to my blindness in one eye I was classified 4-F. When I asked what 4-F meant, I was told that it indicated an applicant who was physically incapable of induction. If something were to happen to the other eye, the army would be responsible for taking care of me for the rest of my life. All Mrs. Newton could do when she found out was say, "Praise the Lord" and laugh and tell me it was going to be okay.

Here I was wearing dresses with my hair in a bun and people actually thought I was holy from my appearance—but my heart was blacker than midnight. I couldn't shake the volcano that erupted within me at unexpected times. Many nights I cried myself to sleep because, no matter how I dressed things up, I still suffered from my past hurts. The nightmares just wouldn't go away and everything I tried seemed to fail.

People told me my past was behind me, but it wasn't. Every time I thought of an incident from my past, I relived the scene all over again with all the anger, hatred, and bitterness. I even felt the physical pain again, even though nothing was being done to me physically. Once, I even looked at my face in a mirror and burst out crying when I saw my blind eye, wishing I was normal like everyone else. I seemed to have created my own monster inside myself.

Mrs. Newton told me I had to forgive those who had hurt me, and I agreed. I called my mother and asked her to forgive me if I had done anything wrong or hurt her in any way. I then asked her why she blinded me. She was the wrong person to ask that question! She shouted, "I never hurt you, that was just your imagination! I didn't blind you. You threw a baby bottle on the floor and it broke, and a piece of glass went into your eye. I didn't do anything to you. Everything was your fault—you never loved me! You're not my child and never will be!" and then slammed the phone down. As I put the phone down in slow motion I cried uncontrollably. If anybody was ready for the funny farm at that point, I was. It was a good thing no one saw the horror that rose up from the depths of my soul at that moment.

I told Mrs. Newton about what happened, but I told her the story in third person because I couldn't be hurt by using the word *we* when disclosing an incident. This went on for many years. The next couple of years were pretty much a blur, but I was still alive—God only knew why. I even wanted God out of the picture because He couldn't seem to protect me, hold me, or even talk to me during that time.

Eventually I went back to wearing pants and I cut my hair. I was told that I would go to hell because I quit wearing dresses and my hair was no longer God's glory. I told them that it was not the clothes that were going to get me into heaven or keep me out of hell, it was my heart. I told them that my long hair looked bad because I never learned how to put it up like other girls and my clothes were tight due to the weight I had gained over the years. No matter what, they never alienated me, but continued to love me—I was never sure why!

In 1984, I received my degree to become a Registered Nurse and began work at the hospital in Gainesville, Florida. While I was in school working toward my degree, one of my teachers told me that I would never pass the medical surgical course. When I asked why, she stated, "Because you're working full time." Her attitude made me all the more determined to prove her wrong. Sure enough, I passed with a B average. As the years went by, I discovered I didn't have to prove anything. All I had to do was the best I was able.

It was about this time that a psychiatric instructor took me under her wing. I was a mess; she had her work cut out for her.

I spent many hours in her office. She stood in the gap for me. I was invited to her family's home, a ranch, to help her around the house or to spend the night. I felt safe at her house, where the demons of my past could not enter. There were horses on the ranch and many times I helped feed the horses or paint the fence with motor oil, which helped to preserve it.

One night, one of the horses had a case of colic and we had to keep the horse standing upright to prevent her from twisting her gut. It happened to have been one of my favorite horses, so we spent the night keeping the horse awake and walking. I went to bed at her house at 6 a.m. The horse made it. It was one of the first accomplishments of my life that really meant something to me.

Fortunately, my next memorable accomplishment came the next morning after taking the nursing exam. I earned my first 100 percent on a test ever. Little by little, my defenses lowered and the bad memories were being replaced by good memories. My psychiatric instructor taught me a lot about what unconditionally loving someone really meant. Her family was becoming my family and the nobody was becoming more of a somebody every day.

I needed to make some extra money so I started selling things at the flea market. It was difficult because I didn't have the guts to tell someone that an item cost more than they were offering to pay. One day, I sold a lady a five-pound bag of pecans. About an hour later, she came back and wanted her money back because she found them a dollar cheaper on another aisle. Instead of haggling with her about the fair price of the item, I ended up giving her money back.

Before I quit the flea market, I met a family named Abbott that was really strange. They laughed and joked and hugged each other all the time. I thought that was weird. They acted like the Newton family that I met a couple of years earlier, except the Abbott's didn't wear dresses or long sleeve shirts all the time. They acted as if they really loved each other.

While chatting with them, tears sometimes welled up in my eyes and I had to ask them to watch my stuff so I could go to the bathroom and get my act together. It seemed so stupid—nobody cries for nothing, but the dirt in my life was unfixable and it felt like I would always be the one-eyed crazy person wherever I went. Who would ever want anyone like that?

This family actually talked to me and joked with me. They didn't think I was crazy. They talked to me about Jesus and how He loved me. They said His blood could wash away my sins and make me clean. I thought I didn't have any sins, I just had hurts and nothing could change that.

One night I was unable to get what they had been saying about how Jesus could make me whole and clean inside. I couldn't wait to see them the next day because they had what I could only wish for—a family. I figured they were just pulling my leg about coming the next day because on the previous day they didn't sell anything. They had no reason to come back. Or did they?

As it turned out, they were true to their word and came back with the same items that hadn't sold the day before. I'd be lying if I told you I wasn't glad to see them. They were the same as they were the day before, and they laughed and talked with each other like always. Their greeting was warm, yet there was something different about them. They invited me to lunch that day. I believed the Abbott's had something I didn't, and I was going to find out what it was.

They invited me to church one Sunday shortly thereafter and I went. The Abbott's had a ministry to kids from all over the world. They lived and taught Jesus every day and ministered to the hurts in the kids' lives. Many people accepted Jesus into their lives, but I was still hurting. I knew I had accepted Jesus into my heart on the last night of that revival meeting. The evangelist had come down the line praying for each person who had responded to that night's altar call. The moment she touched me and began to pray for me, I felt as light as a feather. I cried for the first time in a very long while—and I suddenly knew that I wasn't dirty on the inside anymore, that Jesus cleansed me of my sins. Now I was a messed-up person who had accepted Jesus as my personal Savior, but little by little He helped me become a person again.

I was told that my spirit inside of me was recreated, but that my mind and body had to catch up. Well, my mind and body had a lot of catching up to do. During that period, a lot of changes happened in my mind and in my life—but change takes time.

While I was at the Abbott's home one day, Mrs. Abbott prayed for my leg to grow. I believed it was possible after seeing miracles at the church they went to. Wow! My leg grew almost instantaneously while we were watching! I limped for ten years as a result of my car accident. From that day on, I did not have to wear the ugly built-up shoe, I could wear a regular shoe.

Here I was in my late twenties trying to figure out things I thought I should have learned as a child. I still didn't trust anybody, love was foreign to me, and failure was a part of my daily existence. But I was saved, wasn't I?

I learned that by Jesus' death on the cross, I was cleansed

of my unrighteousness, forgiven for my sins, and that I was bound for heaven, yet my mind and body still had not caught up with my spirit. The Bible said that I had to renew my mind day by day in order to grow and become the person God made me to be. (See Romans 12:2.)

Chapter 9

Abuse hits many families. There is an old saying that goes, "We will not grow beyond that to which we are held bondage and we cannot give away those things we don't possess." Those "things" include a healthy self-image and replacing old hurts with new memories. The problem, however, is in learning how to begin to change when abuse and fear have been a way of life. Change is not easy. When we are caught in a tight spot, we have a tendency to go back to what was comfortable no matter how bad the situation may have actually been. We have memories of both the good and bad things that have happened to us, and we tend to want to keep those memories if we think they are our only treasure in this life. In that comfort zone, we do not have to take responsibility for our behaviors because "They did this to me. It's their fault I am the way I am." *This is wrong!* Each of us controls our choices, both in the present and the future.

I still believed I had the right to hold in contempt those who had hurt me, affected my life, and who took my identity away. When discussing my past, I spoke in the third person, "we." There was no "I" because no "I" existed. The only problem was, as I held the hatred, bitterness, and vengeance in my heart, it caused me to be angry all the time. I used my past as a way to hide my failures because it was my right, or so I thought, to store this garbage I treasured so highly. But the time came to let go of some of my treasured garbage and begin being a person with real feelings and real self-worth.

> *Everyone who has accepted Jesus as their personal Savior is a treasured member of God's family, and He wants us to kick out the dirt in our lives—the lies deeply embedded in our heart and soul.*

Just because a person has a rotten background does not necessarily mean they are locked into a rotten future. When a person leaves an abusive situation, the abuse ends. If they can't leave the abuse in their past, they run the risk of becoming a victim of their own abuse. It won't be an easy road, but there is a starting point where a person begins to take their life back and know they are valuable and special. In other words, they take responsibility for their own life.

When a child is disciplined in most homes, the child is able to be loved by the parent or the person doing the disciplining. An abused child does not know that things are okay again after the discipline. This child grows into an adult who has trouble in jobs and relationships. When constructive criticism is given, they take it personally and become defensive. Most of the time, the person ends up going from job to job due to the unrest in their soul, as well as their lack of the coping skills needed to meet everyday challenges. Unconsciously, they sabotage their jobs so that the old failure syndrome is preserved.

When I realized I didn't have to fail, and that mistakes are not failures if I learned something, I was set free with the knowledge that I can be anything.

No matter how much they may have wanted to be in another family, children of abuse were born to the right family, the family God gave them. No child has the ability to investigate their family before birth. If it was possible, I imagine, most children of abuse would have chosen different families. I wanted a family where there was love instead of hate, where I could have had my education paid for instead of living in my car in order to survive, or especially a Christian family where the love of God flowed from every member of the family. Even though these conditions are not present in every family, we are all special in God's sight. Each of us is a valuable part of the family of God when we have accepted Jesus as our Savior.

Learning to forgive those who hurt you is truly the beginning of freedom from the past.

When as person harbors unforgiveness for others in their heart, they reap the consequences in bad health, broken relationships, and bondage to their emotions. They want the people who hurt them to see and feel their hurt as if they were

Oops! Wrong Family

trying to punish them with their own pain. The other people cannot see their hurt and may not even care. Why do victims of abuse wish to carry a ton of garbage that will, in the end, only destroy them? What do they gain by holding hatred and resentment in their hearts?

The time eventually comes to let the past hurts go through forgiving the person that hurt them. Although they never forget the incidents of the past, they can deal with the feelings that went with them and change the history of their own heart. Complete forgiveness may not come all at once—it is a choice that is made in order to allow the Lord to bring healing in that area of their lives. Eventually there will be a time when that memory of hurt will not evoke the same feelings as when the event occurred. God sends His healing and begins to heal their hurt from the inside out. Little by little, the hurts begin to leave and they find out that if they learned something, then they did not fail.

I have not arrived to full healing quite yet, but I am much more settled in who God says I am instead of who others say I am. When I recall episodes of abuse from my past, the sting and deep hurt are no longer there. Freedom came when I let go of things that hindered me from moving forward, when I exchanged the lie that was embedded in place of the truth.

Forgiving people is a choice—we can choose to stay in bondage and self pity, or we can have life and live it to its fullest (John 10:10). It's not that the abused person is bad, but the choices made are not good, right choices. Decide today, right now, to start making different choices that are choices for the better. We may not have been responsible for the abuse in our past, but we are responsible for choosing the attitude we take in response. If we wish to be truly free,

then we have to take the first step in forgiving others who have hurt us and for things we have done in hurting others. We may just need to forgive ourselves for the wrong choices we have made.

If you have not accepted Jesus as your personal Savior, let me tell you—Jesus died for the brokenhearted and He came to set captives free. On the cross, Jesus paid for our sins forever. By His death, burial, and resurrection we can be made new. His blood covers all of our sins. No matter what you have done to others, or what others have done to you, there is healing in Jesus.

If you want to accept Jesus as your Savior, just ask Him:

Lord Jesus,

I believe You died for my sins and I want You to forgive me for my sins. I accept You as my Savior. Help me to live for You and to get to know You better. Help me forgive those who have hurt me, and I ask Your forgiveness for the hurt I have caused others. Help me to forgive myself for the wrong choices I have made. Please come into my heart, Lord, and fill me with Your love. Amen.

When asking for forgiveness for those who have hurt you, you may want to write down the people involved as well as the incidents. You might even verbally speak their names and the incidents involved.

If you do not believe Jesus can save you and make you whole, just try Him. Just say, "God, if You are really out there, make Yourself real to me." He never turns away those who earnestly seek Him.

When you go to the person in question and ask them to

forgive you, they may not accept your apology. When you tell someone that you forgive them for hurting you, they may give you more grief. We all need to be free, whether the other person desires the same for their life or not. Real freedom comes from faith in Jesus, which will lead you to truly forgiving others.

Epilogue

In July 2005, I visited my mother for the first time in many years. We spoke little, and our time together was short. A few weeks later, she passed away after a very brief bout with cancer. My sister later told me that the one person my mother asked to see before she died was me. I don't know if she wanted some form of reconciliation, but I hoped then as I do now that my presence helped her make peace with God before she died.

Nobody said life would be a bed of roses. There are many thorns along the stem—but at the end there is a beautiful flower. Our past does not have to destroy our future. You do not have to be a victim of the abuse of your past. If you prayed the prayer before and asked Jesus into your life, then find a church where you will be able to grow. Get a Bible and start reading in the Book of John for starters, and allow the Holy Spirit to guide you into His truth.

About the Author

DEBI TOPOROFF WAS born in Stuart, Florida. She was graduated from Santa Fe Community College with an associate's degree in nursing and has been in the mental health field for over thirty years. She received her bachelor's degree in sociology from the University of South Carolina in 1996, and a master's degree in health services administration in 1998 from Central Michigan University. At the Life School of Theology, Debi earned a master's degree in theology, and a doctor of ministry degree. She also holds a specialized associate's degree in legal nurse counseling from the School of Paralegal Services in Boca Raton, Florida. She has one daughter and currently lives in Beech Island, South Carolina.